101 Celtic
BORDERS

101 Celtic
BORDERS

courtney davis

David and Charles

A DAVID & CHARLES BOOK
Copyright © David & Charles Limited 2007

David & Charles is an F+W Publications Inc. company
4700 East Galbraith Road
Cincinnati, OH 45236

First published in the UK in 2007

Text and illustrations copyright © Courtney Davis 2007

A catalogue record for this book is available from the
British Library.

ISBN-13: 978-0-7153-2433-2
ISBN-10: 0-7153-2433-0

Printed in Malaysia by KHL Printing Co Sdn Bhd
for David & Charles
Brunel House   Newton Abbot   Devon

Commissioning Editor   Neil Baber
Assistant Editor   Louise Clark
Design Assistant   Eleanor Stafford
Production Controller   Kelly Smith

Visit our website at **www.davidandcharles.co.uk**

David & Charles books are available from all good bookshops;
alternatively you can contact our Orderline on 0870 9908222
or write to us at FREEPOST EX2 110, D&C Direct, Newton
Abbot, TQ12 4ZZ (no stamp required UK only); US customers
call 800-289-0963 and Canadian customers call 800-840-5220.

*This book is dedicated to the scribes
of the past whose artistry is still such
a creative inspiration to us today, and
to all the would-be Celtic artists in
the future, may your pens and brushes
run true.*

*Special thanks to Neil Baber for his valuable
input on the introduction and his help on the
rest of the 101 Celtic books.*

contents

introduction

The development of what could be called decorative 'borders' in the Celtic manner did not occur until the early Christian or Insular period, between the 6th and 9th centuries AD, principally in the monastic centres of Ireland, Scotland and Northumbria. This was the era of the high style of Celtic art, when it was fully developed in its many intricacies and characteristic motifs. It was applied to manuscript copies of the sacred gospel texts, which were embellished with ornamented initials and miniatures, intricate painted decoration that sometimes occupied entire pages (known as 'carpet pages') and, in many cases, with decorative borders.

However, long before the creation of the gospel books of the Christian period, Celtic peoples had been using patterns and ornaments to decorate stone crosses and slabs, as well as jewellery and other items crafted in metal, wood and bone. We know that the pre-Christian Celts indulged their love of colour and ornament in designs for painted wood, embroidery and decorated leatherwork, and we can presume that such decoration enriched many other aspects of their lives, though little of this remains beyond a few tantalizing glimpses, mainly of jewellery and metalwork such as the 7th-century Tara brooch found in Co. Meath, Ireland, and the treasures of the Sutton Hoo burial site in Suffolk, England.

While the exquisitely worked ornament on such pieces demonstrates how much the pagan Celts delighted in such embellishments, it also appears to show an aversion to decorative voids, since the complex and intertwining ornamentation expands to fill every available space. This is the tradition and background to the style that was developed and perfected by the great monastic artists, taking the decorative components of their art – knotwork, spirals, key patterns and zoomorphic designs – and creating seemingly impossibly intricate and beautiful embellishments in vivid colours on the pages of their sacred books.

The first two chapters of this book take designs from these earlier periods, found in decorative schemes on stone and metal artifacts, and use the motifs and patterns to construct decorative borders, giving them a modern application. The third chapter looks at the greatest achievement of Celtic art – the famous illuminated manuscripts of the early Christian period in Britain – and includes border designs inspired by them.

The Era of Manuscript Illumination

Like that of the pre-Christian period, the reputation of the great era of manuscript illumination rests on relatively few extant examples. The earliest surviving manuscript is a psalter known as the Cathach of St Columba. It was probably executed between the late 6th and early 7th centuries and shows simple decorations around the initial letters, drawn in the same brown and red inks that are used for the script. Many of the letters are further embellished by an outline of red dots. The lettering shows a clear connection with that of the somewhat later Book of Durrow (possibly the oldest surviving complete gospel book produced in Britain or Ireland), pointing to a shared tradition of the monks who completed the two books.

Although little remains of the Durham Gospel Fragment, it contains the earliest example of interlace decoration – on the colophon page at the end of the Gospel of St Matthew, and it is also the earliest surviving Celtic painted manuscript. Interlace or knotwork was primarily used as a filler in Celtic decoration, since the weaving ribbons could be manipulated to fit most spaces, and it is a key characteristic of the style. In manuscripts the artist would execute the technique by pricking small dots into the paper or vellum to use as a guide and then create ribbons passing over, under and around them. The use of vellum fostered the development of painted decoration, as its suede-like surface was highly receptive to coloured inks.

Another 7th-century manuscript kept at Durham Cathedral Library, known as the Durham Gospels, is a second and more substantial fragment of a large gospel book, completed within a few years of the Fragment. The Durham Gospels show a radical change, in that the simple knotwork borders of the earlier book have been transformed into a mass of interwoven animals and lace-like plaited knots.

The 8th century is now considered to mark the beginning of the golden age of Celtic art, not just in manuscript illumination but in all areas of craftsmanship, because of its skilled execution and the precision of the detail in works such as the Tara brooch (an exquisitely worked piece with gold, silver, amber and glass inlays and knotwork decoration) and the Ardagh chalice (a large and intricately decorated silver cup). Like the Tara brooch, the chalice was discovered in a hoard hidden from Viking raiders and is now in the collection of the National Museum of Ireland.

In the field of manuscript decoration, the monastery founded in 635 by St Aidan on the island of Lindisfarne, off the coast of Northumbria, had an important part to play. The Lindisfarne Gospels, which were produced there in the late 7th or early 8th century, mark a new development in style, employing intricate panels of zoomorphic designs, often entwined with knotwork. Birds, for example, have realistic features such as hooked bills and sharp claws, reminiscent of birds of prey or the cormorants found on Lindisfarne (also known as Holy Island). The illuminated pages are designed with great complexity and imagination but also have a geometric regularity and balance and display exquisite workmanship.

Perhaps even more famous, the Book of Kells is the most ornate of the surviving Celtic manuscripts, representing a quality of workmanship that would not be equalled. The full-page decorations in this work are separate from the main body of text – perhaps so that several pages could be worked on simultaneously, with apprentices filling in the less demanding details. This would also have given the monks control over the selection of pages for the final bound book, allowing them to include only those of the highest quality. The detail is so intricate that it can hardly be seen without the aid of a magnifying glass, leading to the conclusion that some sort of glass or crystal must have been used to aid the artists. The *Chi Rho* page in particular includes tiny images of animals, such as butterflies and an otter biting a fish, and many other details that are hardly visible when viewing the page as a whole.

The book was probably begun on the monastic island of Iona, off the west coast of Scotland, where a missionary centre was established by St Columba in the mid-6th century. However, it was later moved to keep it safe from the constant Viking raids around the British coast that began at the end of the 8th century. The monasteries could put up little defence against the marauding Vikings, and many communities were forced to flee to Europe. The precious volume was taken, along with the relics of St Columba, to a new monastery at Kells in Ireland, where it was completed in 807.

The Decorative Components

Celtic design relies on a range of repeated motifs to build up its decorative effect. The spiral occurs in primitive forms in many early cultures, no doubt inspired by the natural patterns of growth that occur repeatedly in nature, such as in shells, animal horns and plants. It is perhaps no surprise, therefore, that spiral designs are found in the earliest examples of Celtic art. Spirals appear on the stones of Newgrange in Ireland, thought to have been built around 3200 BC. So-called 'key patterns' are similar to spirals in formation but squared off, and they bear a strong resemblance to decorative styles used by early peoples all over the world. There is no mistaking the similarity of these devices to the fretwork patterning characteristic of classical Greek and Roman design, but also to the decorative motifs of the Maya in Central America, which are still associated with the culture of that part of the world. Elements of Chinese art demonstrate similar designs. Key patterns found on mammoth tusk carvings from Eastern Europe perhaps point to contacts between migrating peoples at an early date, which may explain some of the similarities.

The next stage of pattern development was the interlace or knotwork that is so characteristic of Celtic art. It has been suggested that this style of decoration was introduced to Britain and Ireland from Coptic Egypt, as there are parallels between Celtic manuscripts and the scribal techniques of the early Coptic Christians, but it is also true that interlaced designs based upon basketwork and plaiting are common to the ornament of many early cultures.

The addition of zoomorphic and anthropomorphic elements became increasingly prevalent during the period of monastic manuscript illumination, particularly the inclusion of symbolic animals and figures such as the symbols of the four evangelists: lion, eagle, ox and man. By the 10th and 11th centuries, with the growing influence of Scandinavia on Celtic art, spirals and key patterns started to disappear from the decoration and the beasts became even more stylized and ribbon-like. With the increased pressure on the scribes to produce more books to serve the growing demand of the expanding Church, the style deteriorated somewhat and the creative fervour that had produced the earlier elaborately decorated books waned. The only manuscripts that have survived from the 10th and 11th centuries are psalters and copies of St Jerome's second revision of the Latin text of the psalms, known as the Gallican version.

Using the Designs

In the 101 examples of decorative borders in this book, I have tried to draw on designs representing the entire history and development of Celtic art. There are endless possibilities for creative expression, and the final chapter contains some examples of my own 'modern' border designs – new interpretations inspired by the genius of the Celtic artists and craftsmen. Many of the borders have repeating patterns, so the designs can be easily extended to make decorated frames of any size. I hope they will also inspire you to adapt and create your own Celtic designs and join the great tradition of this sublime art.

designs in stone

one

Spiral pattern from an 8th-century cross slab. *Woodwray, Angus, Scotland*

two

Key pattern carved on an 8th-century cross slab. *Clonmacnois, Co. Offaly, Ireland*

Knotwork border from the Rossie Priory stone of the mid-8th century.
Rossie Priory, Perth and Kinross, Scotland

designs in stone

Step pattern border adapted from a 9th-century carved stone cross.
Ahenny, Co. Tipperary, Ireland

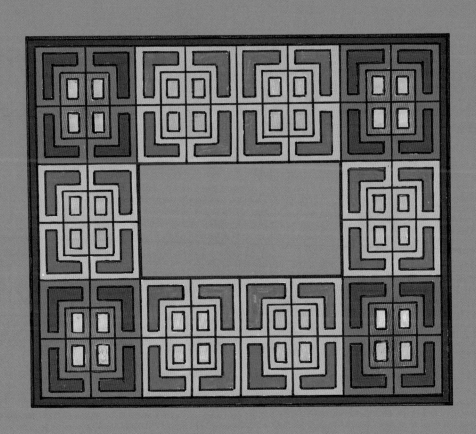

Design from a section of the shaft of the 4m (13ft) Carew pillar cross.
Nevern, Pembrokeshire, Wales

Key pattern from a panel on a cross slab. *Rosemarkie, Ross and Cromarty, Scotland*

The Tree of Life pattern on the 8th-century St Vigean's stone cross slab is thought to have been copied from an illuminated manuscript that is now lost. *Arbroath, Angus, Scotland*

Knotwork border adapted from a pattern on a pillar cross dated around the 10th century.
Nevern, Pembrokeshire, Wales

Border taken from an 8th-century stone fragment.
St Mary's Church, Lastingham, North Yorkshire, England

designs in stone

Fretwork pattern adapted from the richly decorated 9th-century Nigg cross slab.
Nigg, Ross and Cromarty, Scotland

eleven

Border created from a single knotwork panel on the cross shaft of the 8th-century
Kirk of Norham cross. *Norham, Northumberland, England*

Tree of Life pattern from a 7th–8th-century stone fragment.
Hexham, Northumberland, England

Border design carved on the shaft of the 8th-century cross of the Kirk of Norham.
Norham, Northumberland, England

fourteen

Design from a 9th-century panel on the highly decorative Nigg stone, a superb blend of high- and low-relief decorative carving. *Nigg, Ross and Cromarty, Scotland*

fifteen

Knotwork from a late 9th-century cross shaft. *Monifieth, Angus, Scotland*

Border design from a panel on an 8th-century cross slab.
Rosemarkie, Ross and Cromarty, Scotland

Knotwork interlace from an 8th-century cross slab panel. The panel is sometimes called a 'page of stone' as it is thought to represent a page from a gospel book.
Rossie Priory, Perth and Kinross, Scotland

Key pattern design from an 8th-century cross slab that was found to have been built into the wall of St Andrew's Cathedral around 1160. *St Andrews, Fife, Scotland*

Key pattern design from a richly carved pictorial cross slab from the 8th century.
Meigle, Perth and Kinross, Scotland

Interlace from the 8th-century Rossie Priory stone.
Rossie Priory, Perth and Kinross, Scotland

twenty–one

Design from a 7th–8th-century stone fragment. *Spital, Hexham, Northumberland, England*

twenty-two

Arrowhead key pattern from the 8th-century Nigg stone.
Nigg, Ross and Cromarty, Scotland

twenty~three

Viking-influenced design from the late 9th-century Gosforth cross.
Gosforth, Cumbria, England

twency~four

Border adapted from a late 9th-century cross slab. *Woodwray, Angus, Scotland*

Border created from an intricate key pattern carved on the panel of an 8th-century cross slab. *Rosemarkie, Ross and Cromarty, Scotland*

Pattern taken from an 8th-century cross slab that was relegated in 1160 to the foundations of St Andrew's Cathedral. *St Andrews, Fife, Scotland*

twenty~seven

Ring chain pattern showing the influence of the Viking Borre style on the late 9th-century Gosforth cross. *Gosforth, Cumbria, England*

twenty-eight

Key pattern from the 8th-century Nigg stone, noted for its pronounced bosses and intricate detail. *Nigg, Ross and Cromarty, Scotland*

twenty–nine

Tree of Life design from a stone fragment. *Abercorn, Northumberland, England*

designs in metalwork and ivory

designs in metalwork and ivory

Border from a copper alloy and enamel hanging bowl dated around the 7th century.
Scunthorpe Museum, North Lincolnshire, England

Bronze trumpet mouthpiece dated between 100 BC and 100 AD. The running wave pattern terminates in boss end spirals. *National Museum of Ireland, Dublin*

designs in metalwork and ivory

Simple knotwork border from bronze and silver plates found on the 8th-century
house-shaped Monymusk reliquary, which once contained the relic of St Columba.
National Museum of Scotland, Edinburgh

thirty-three

Spiral decoration from a bronze scabbard of 200 BC. *British Museum, London*

thirty-four

Knotwork from the 8th-century Tara brooch, which is considered to be the finest surviving example of Celtic penannualar brooches. *National Museum of Ireland, Dublin*

designs in metalwork and ivory

The 8th century was the golden age of Celtic art and the gilt-bronze Tara brooch is one of the finest examples from that period. *National Museum of Ireland, Dublin*

designs in metalwork and ivory

Scroll design from a bronze object dated 350–300 BC.
Museum für Urgeschichte des Landes Niederösterreich, Asparn an der Zaya, Austria

thirty~seven

Knotwork from the 8th-century Monymusk reliquary, the only example of this type of shrine to survive more or less intact in Britain. *National Museum of Scotland, Edinburgh*

thirty-eight

Simple knotwork border from the Genoels-Elderen diptych of the late 8th century.
Musées Royaux d'Art et d'Histoire, Brussels

Patternwork from the Ardagh chalice, one of the finest examples of 8th-century Irish metalwork. *National Museum of Ireland, Dublin*

Spiral design from the 6th-century Romano-Celtic Ipswich hanging bowl.
British Museum, London

forty-one

Design from the 8th-century Ardagh chalice. *National Museum of Ireland, Dublin*

designs in metalwork and ivory

Design from an 8th–9th century Irish harness mount made from copper alloy and gilt and found in Sandnes, Rogaland, Norway. *Universitetets Oldsaksamling, Oslo*

designs in illuminated manuscripts

forty-three

Border design from the omega of the León Bible of 960.
Collegiate Church of San Isidoro, León, Spain

Forty~Four

Panel design from the Lindisfarne Gospels, thought to have been created by Eadfrith, who later became Bishop of Lindisfarne in 698 AD. *British Library, London*

forty–five

Interlaced panel from the late 7th-century Book of Durrow. *Trinity College, Dublin*

forty-six

Tree of Life pattern from the early 9th-century Book of Kells, the most famous of all the Insular manuscripts and the pinnacle of Celtic draughtsmanship. *Trinity College, Dublin*

Knotwork and spiral pattern from the 9th-century Book of Kells.
Trinity College, Dublin

Forty-eight

The number three was an important symbol for both pagan and Christian Celts, signifying both the triple figure of maiden, mother and crone and the Holy Trinity. This triple spiral pattern is taken from the Book of Kells. *Trinity College, Dublin*

Adapted continuous knotwork pattern from the 12th-century Armagh Gospel.
British Library, London

Knotwork design from the late 7th-century Book of Durrow, the earliest surviving fully illuminated gospel book. *Trinity College, Dublin*

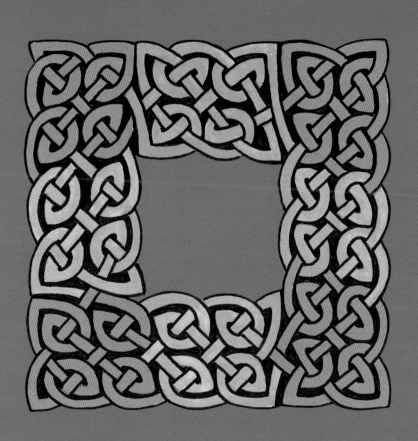

fifty one

Panel design from the late 7th-century Lindisfarne Gospels, dedicated to St Cuthbert and thought to have been produced by Eadfrith for his own use. *British Library, London*

fifty-two

Knotwork border design from the late 7th-century Book of Durrow adapted into a circle.
Trinity College, Dublin

fifty-three

Tree of Life pattern taken from a panel in the Book of Kells. *Trinity College, Dublin*

fifty~four

Spiral border from the Book of Kells. *Trinity College, Dublin*

fifty-five

Knotwork border taken from a medallion in the Book of Kells. *Trinity College, Dublin*

The Tree of Life growing from a pot, from the Book of Kells. *Trinity College, Dublin*

Design from the Book of Kells. The pattern has similarities to a design on the earlier Ardagh chalice. *Trinity College, Dublin*

fifty-eight

Spirals from the Book of Kells. *Trinity College, Dublin*

fifty-nine

Key pattern from the Book of Kells. *Trinity College, Dublin*

Knotwork design from the Book of Durrow, which may have been executed by Eadfrith, the artist who created the Lindisfarne Gospels. *Trinity College, Dublin*

sixty~one

A double spiral border design from the Book of Kells. *Trinity College, Dublin*

sixty-two

Knotwork pattern taken from the Book of Kells, with similarities to designs in the earlier
Book of Durrow. *Trinity College, Dublin*

sixty~three

A border design from the Book of Kells based on double and triple spirals.
Trinity College, Dublin

sixty–four

Knotwork from the Book of Durrow. The work is thought to have been produced in a Columban monastery, though whether in Ireland, Iona or Northumbria is uncertain. *Trinity College, Dublin*

Adapted continuous knotwork pattern from the 12th-century Armagh Gospel.
British Library, London

Knotwork border design from the Book of Durrow. *Trinity College, Dublin*

sixty~seven

Spiral border, with knotwork links between swirls, from the Book of Kells.
Trinity College, Dublin

Key pattern border from the Book of Kells. *Trinity College, Dublin*

Simple squared-off knotwork border design from the Book of Durrow.
Trinity College, Dublin

Knotwork panel design from the Book of Durrow. The pattern is similar to a design on the later, Viking-influenced Gosforth stone cross. *Trinity College, Dublin*

seventy–one

Interlaced key pattern from the Book of Kells. *Trinity College, Dublin*

seventy-two

Border from the Book of Kells. *Trinity College, Dublin*

Border from the Book of Kells. *Trinity College, Dublin*

seventy-four

Border from the Book of Kells. A similar key pattern appears on the 8th-century Rosemarkie cross slab. *Trinity College, Dublin*

Interlaced pattern from the Lindisfarne Gospels. *British Library, London*

Knotwork design from the Book of Durrow. *Trinity College, Dublin*

Double banded knotwork interlace from the Book of Durrow. *Trinity College, Dublin*

Interlace border from the Book of Durrow. *Trinity College, Dublin*

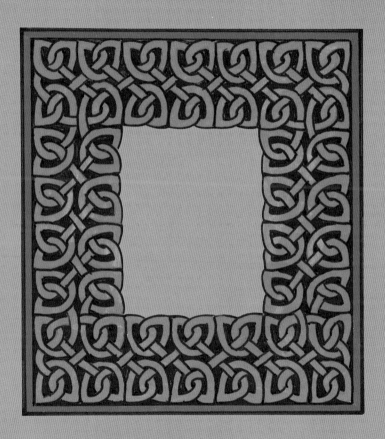

designs in illuminated manuscripts

Border from the Book of Durrow. *Trinity College, Dublin*

The Book of Durrow is noted for the interesting variety of styles in its knotwork.
Trinity College, Dublin

designs in illuminated manuscripts

Border from the Book of Durrow. *Trinity College, Dublin*

eighty-two

Border adapted from a design in the Book of Durrow, with similarities to patterns in the Viking Borre style. *Trinity College, Dublin*

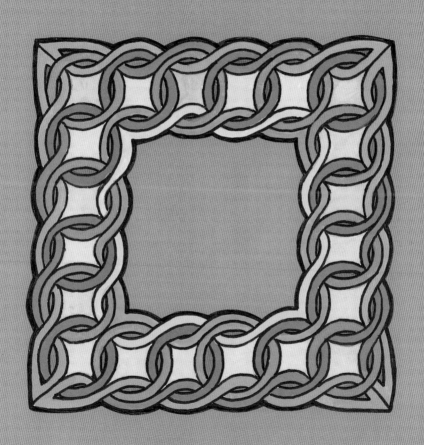

eighty~three

Key pattern from the Lindisfarne Gospels. *British Library, London*

designs in illuminated manuscripts

Border design from the Book of Kells. *Trinity College, Dublin*

eighty–five

Panel design from the Lindisfarne Gospels. *British Library, London*

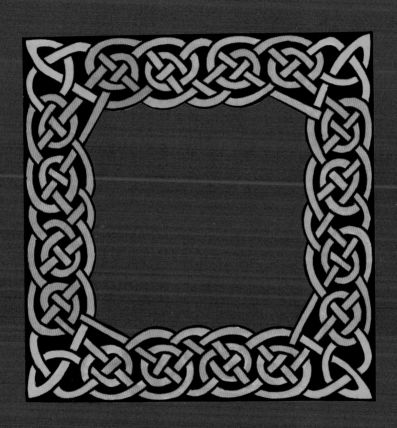

eighty~six

Knotwork frame from the Book of Durrow. *Trinity College, Dublin*

designs in illuminated manuscripts

Border from the Book of Durrow. *Trinity College, Dublin*

Border from the Book of Durrow. *Trinity College, Dublin*

eighty–nine

Design from the Lindisfarne Gospels. *British Library, London*

modern designs

Border of entwined men from my book *St Patrick, a Visual Celebration* (1999).

Border built up using the diamond and the swastika (an ancient symbol of lightning).

modern designs

The spiral symbolizes the continuous movement of spirit from one form of existence to another.

ninety–three

Border adapted from a design on the 8th-century Hilton of Cadboll stone.
Ross and Cromarty, Scotland

Knotwork symbolizes the sacred thread that binds us all.

Border design created from various sources.

Raised serpent knotwork border.

ninety~seven

Knotwork fire.

Another border adapted from a design on the 8th-century Hilton of Cadboll stone.
Ross and Cromarty, Scotland

Triple spiral border.

one hundred

Knotwork border taken from various sources.

one hundred and one

Design based on a Chinese button knot, traditionally tied by Chinese tailors to make buttons for clothes. When the knot is pulled tight it forms a ball.

Books by Courtney Davis

The Celtic Saints,
Blandford Press, 1995

The Celtic Image,
Blandford Press, 1996

Celtic Ornament: The Art of the Scribe,
Blandford Press, 1996

Celtic Initials and Alphabets,
Blandford Press, 1997

Celtic Illumination: The Irish School,
Thames & Hudson, 1998

Celtic Tattoo: Workbook One,
Awen Press, 2002

Celtic Tattoo: Workbook Two,
Awen Press, 2003

Viking Tattoo: Workbook,
Awen Press, 2003

More information and examples of the art of Courtney Davis
can be found at: **www.celtic-art.com**